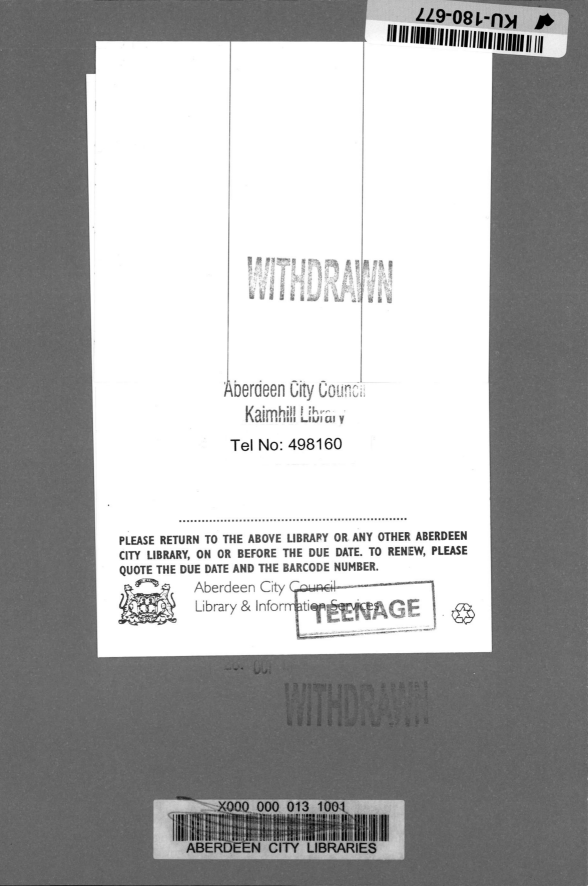

Teen Issues

DIET

Joanna Kedge and Joanna Watson

R **www.raintreepublishers.co.uk**
Visit our website to find out more information about **Raintree** books.

To order:
☎ Phone 44 (0) 1865 888113
▤ Send a fax to 44 (0) 1865 314091
▢ Visit the Raintree Bookshop at **www.raintreepublishers.co.uk** to browse our catalogue and order online.

First published in Great Britain by
Raintree, Halley Court,
Jordan Hill, Oxford OX2 8EJ, part of
Harcourt Education.
Raintree is a registered trademark of Harcourt
Education Ltd.

Editorial: Charlotte Guillain
and Kate Buckingham
Design: Michelle Lisseter
and Tinstar Design Ltd (www.tinstar.co.uk)
Picture Research: Mica Brancic
Production: Jonathan Smith
Index: Indexing Specialists (UK) Ltd

Originated by Dot Gradations
Printed and bound in China by South China
Printing Company

ISBN 1 844 43146 0
08 07 06 05 04
10 9 8 7 6 5 4 3 2 1

British Library Cataloguing in Publication Data
Kedge, Joanna and Watson, Joanna
Diet
613.2
A full catalogue record for this book is available from
the British Library.

Acknowledgements
The publishers would like to thank the following for
permission to reproduce photographs: Alamy pp.
24–25, 30–31, 38–39; Bubbles pp. 4, 6, 15, 22–23,
27; Bubbles pp. 36–37 (Pauline Cutler); Corbis pp. 5,
6, 7, 10–11, 12, 14, 16, 18, 21, 23, 25, 26–27, 29, 31,
37, 38, 42, 44-45, 49, 50–51; Gareth Boden pp. i, 13,
30; Getty pp. 18–19; Getty pp. 22, 32, 44, 46–47, 48
(PhotoDisc); Getty p. 24 (Stone); Getty pp. 4, 32–33,
36 (Taxi); John Birdsall pp. 4–5, 6, 40, 45; Richard
Greenhill pp. 10, 12–13; SPL pp. 5, 6, 17, 34–35,
40–41, 43; Trevor Clifford p. 11; Tudor Photography
pp. 14–15, 16–17, 28–29, 42–43, 46.

Cover photograph of hamburgers on scales
reproduced with permission of Corbis (Mark Cooper).

The paper used to print this book comes from
sustainable resources.

613.2

Contents

Any words appearing in the text in bold,
like this, are explained in the Glossary.
You can also look out for them in the 'In the
know' box at the bottom of each page.

Food and drink

It's okay to eat chocolate, but just not too much.

I know I eat too many chips, but I eat lots of fruit and vegetables too.

I have to watch what I eat, because I have put on weight.

All food and drink affects the body in some way – sometimes in good ways and sometimes in not so good ways. As you go through changes in your teens, you may feel more aware of your body and how it looks and feels. It is likely that you and your friends are not growing at the same rate and you all look very different. You may not even like the way you feel or look and become worried about how much you weigh or whether other people think that you are attractive. One way to feel really good about yourself is to be careful about the food you eat.

Why can't I eat whatever I like?

organs   internal parts of your body that are essential for you to stay alive, such as heart, lungs and kidneys

We all need food and water to survive. Healthy food can make a real difference to your body shape, your skin, your weight and even your moods. Food also affects what goes on inside your body. It can make a difference to how well your heart works and how strong your bones and joints are. Without certain foods you may develop illnesses. What we drink also affects **organs** such as the liver and kidneys. We all need to eat and drink carefully to make sure we are as healthy and happy as possible.

How come my friends look so much better than me?

How can I lose weight and be the shape I want to be?

Find out later...

How can you have a healthy lifestyle?

What are eating disorders and what can you do if you have one?

Why is junk food so bad for you?

Why do we eat?

❝ There are lots of reasons people choose to eat. Food gives us energy and keeps our bodies in good working order. You need to make sure you eat a variety of food types because each one helps a different part of your body. ❞

Food provides fuel for our bodies and helps us to keep active. It gives us energy and can help us feel fit and good about ourselves. Our bodies tell us when we need more food by making us feel hungry, weak and tired. However, feeling hungry is not the only reason we eat. Here are some other reasons:

I always eat more when I'm bored and fed up. I don't know why, but I think it makes me feel better. It gives me something to do!

I eat loads of fruit. Someone told me that it's good for my skin. I think it must be because my skin is really clear. Sometimes I get the odd spot, but that's ok, it's normal. My favourite fruit is mango.

digest   to break food down in the stomach, so that it can be absorbed into the blood

I try to eat something like a bowl of pasta about four hours before I play football. That way the food has time to **digest** and is stored as energy. It makes me play better and I can run around for longer.

Sometimes I eat even when I'm not hungry, just because the food is there. My mum says I'm greedy. I say I love food.

'It is good to have three meals a day.'

TRUE

It is important that you have three good meals a day. They will keep you from feeling hungry and give you plenty of energy. Breakfast is a really good start to the day.

Nutrition Facts

Amount per serving

Calories 100

Calories from Fat 0

% Daily Value

Total Fat 0g	0%
Saturated Fat 0g	0%
Cholesterol 0g	0%
Sodium 60mg	3%
Total Carbohydrate 0g	7%
Sugars 15g	
Protein 3g	

Labels

You will find labels on all packaged food. Look at them carefully to find out how much energy, fat and sugar the food contains.

A balanced diet

It is important to eat lots of different types of food. A good mix will help keep you healthy – this is called having a **balanced diet**. During your teens, it is important to know the value of different foods, for example, which foods might give you spots and which will help keep your skin clear. At the moment, your body is going through lots of changes. You need a balanced diet to help you grow healthily. One of the most important things you can do is to drink lots of water everyday.

> **Fruit and vegetables:** these look after the whole of your body, your blood, skin and general health. They should be the second biggest part of your diet.

> **Carbohydrates:** these foods are good for giving you lots of energy. They should make up the biggest part of the food you eat.

balanced diet   eating a good range and mixture of foods from all the different food groups

Fats and sugars: some fat in your diet is essential but your body does not need too much of this food type. Many foods rich in fat and sugar might give you instant energy but should only be eaten as part of a balanced diet.

Proteins: these build muscle and help repair your body. They will help you grow and have a more shapely body. You should eat protein everyday.

Q&A

Q I am trying to lose weight and so I only eat salad. Is this balanced?

A Take a look at this food pyramid. The foods at the top of the pyramid should be eaten the least. The foods at the bottom you should try and eat the most of. It is good to eat lots of fruit and vegetables, but you need other foods too, especially energy foods like pasta and rice.

carbohydrates foods such as bread, potatoes, rice and cereals that provide the body with a source of energy

Energy foods

Carbohydrates is the food group that gives you energy. You can get them from bread, cereals, rice, pasta and potatoes. Carbohydrates should make up the largest part of your diet. A diet without them will leave you feeling tired and weak.

Julia, aged 16, has been on a diet without carbohydrates for nearly 3 weeks now. This is a diet where you can eat lots of meat, cheese and fried food, but hardly any bread, pasta, rice or potatoes. You are not even allowed to eat much fruit.

Did you know?

Chips are a good source of carbohydrate because they are made of potato. However, they also contain a lot of fat. You need to be careful how you cook your food. Potatoes are better for you if they are boiled or baked, rather than fried to make chips.

vitamins   chemicals that the body needs to stay healthy

Julia says that she has lost a bit of weight, but she feels very unhealthy and is tired all the time.

' At first I loved eating fatty food like fried eggs, bacon and cheese. But I started craving bread and pasta. '

Julia has found it difficult to exercise over the last three weeks because she feels so weak. She has decided to stop the diet.

' I would rather go back to healthy eating and be sure that I am eating a balanced diet. I want to get all my **vitamins** and protein and hopefully I will regain my energy. '

Doctors do not advise people to go on this diet because carbohydrates are a vital part of a **balanced diet**.

Carbohydrates

You should try to eat about six servings of foods rich in carbohydrates each day.

Food	How much is a serving?
bread or toast	one large slice
rice	half a cup
potatoes	two small
pasta	half a cup
muffin	one medium sized

▶ All these foods are rich in carbohydrates.

Growth foods

Fit food

I have always been fast, which is what makes me a good athlete, but I am not naturally strong. I used to have trouble keeping up with training. Luckily, my coach advised me to eat lots of meat and dairy products, as well as **carbohydrates**, and fruit and vegetables. This helped my body build the muscle I needed. No one can stop me now!

To... | Doctor
Cc... |
Subject: | Weedy

Dear Doctor,
I am smaller than everyone in my class at school, and they all seem to be stronger and have more muscles than me. I feel like such a weed. Am I normal? Is there anything I can do?
Aaron

To... | Aaron
Cc... |
Subject: | Weedy

Dear Aaron,
Don't worry, you're completely normal. During your teenage years, you all grow at different speeds – it just takes longer for some people than for others. Make sure you have lots of protein in your diet, such as meat, fish, eggs, nuts and beans – this will help your body grow.

pulses   seeds of plants such as peas, beans and lentils, which are eaten as food

To... Coach

Cc...

Subject: Protein pills

Dear Coach,
I am mad about baseball. A friend has told me that I should start taking protein pills to make me stronger and fitter. Are they safe and will they work?
Serena

To... Serena

Cc...

Subject: Protein pills

Dear Serena,
Protein **supplements** can be very dangerous. They are supposed to give the body artificial doses of proteins to make you grow. But these supplements are not tested to see if they are safe, so you could be taking something dangerous. The best way of increasing your fitness is to train more, get plenty of sleep, eat a **balanced diet** and drink lots of water.

TRUE OR FALSE?

'People who are vegetarians cannot get protein from their diet.'

FALSE

Vegetarians can get their protein from dairy foods, eggs, nuts, beans and **pulses**.

> > > > > > > > > > >

Go to page 44 to find out more about a vegetarian diet.

supplements   tablets or drinks taken to enhance certain parts of your diet
vegetarian   someone who chooses not to eat fish or meat

Your body needs fifteen different vitamins every day.

You should eat at least five portions of fruit and vegetables every day.

A carrot, a small glass of orange juice, a small bunch of grapes, a large slice of mango and a small bowl of salad are each a single portion size.

Good health

You get **vitamins** and **minerals** from the food you eat, and they help keep your body healthy and fight off illness. There are lots of different types of vitamins and minerals and each one does a different job. Vitamins and minerals are natural substances that are found in many foods. Minerals can be found in milk, water, cheese, fresh fish and green and leafy vegetables. Vitamins are found in fresh fruit and vegetables. The table below shows where some vitamins are found and what they do.

Foods	Vitamin	Needed for...
Carrots and fish	A	healthy eyes and skin
Spinach, nuts and **pulses**	B	healthy nerves and skin
Strawberries and oranges	C	healthy blood and gums
Eggs and milk	D	strong bones and teeth
Nuts and avocados	E	healthy cells and skin
Broccoli and peas	K	clotting blood

minerals   simple substances found naturally in the Earth – they can help build your body and keep it healthy

To... Doctor
Cc...
Subject: Spots

Dear Doctor,
I have got loads of spots on my face and back and I find them really embarrassing. I try to keep my skin really clean and I don't even eat chocolate. What can I do to get rid of them? Please help me.

James

To... James
Cc...
Subject: Spots

Dear James,
You are doing all the right things. You need to wash carefully and watch what you eat. Vitamins help to keep you healthy and foods like spinach, nuts and **pulses** contain a lot of vitamin B which is good for your skin. You must remember that you are not alone. Many teenagers suffer from spots – you will grow out of it!

Take care.

Q I keep getting colds and often feel really rough. Is there anything I can do to stop this?

A People often feel run down if they don't get enough vitamins in their diet. This means they can become ill more easily. Make sure you are eating plenty of fresh fruit and vegetables.

Chocolate and chips

Some types of food give you very few **nutrients** or goodness but are still really tasty. Foods like this contain a lot of fats and sugars and should only be eaten in small amounts. Eating too many of these foods may cause **obesity** which can make it more difficult for your body to work properly. Always check the fat and sugar content on food packages.

Sweets

My cousin eats loads of chips, and he has started putting on weight.

There's nothing in sweets and chocolates really – they just make you fat.

I love sweets, but I know I need to clean and floss my teeth after eating them.

These are full of sugar, which can make you put on weight if not eaten as part of a healthy **balanced diet**. The drinks that promise to give you lots of energy really just give you a rush of sugar. The best drink for your body is water.

cholesterol   fatty substance made by the body that can block the arteries to and from the heart

These foods are full of a fat called **saturated fat**, which makes the body form too much **cholesterol**. The fats that your body needs are called **polyunsaturated fat** and **monounsaturated fat** – these can be found in vegetable oils, such as olive oil and in oily fish. These oils provide the body with warmth and some energy, but do not build up cholesterol in the blood.

Dentist
If you do have lots of sweets and sugary drinks, make sure you clean your teeth at least twice a day and floss to get rid of any **plaque**.

▲ The blue areas in this photo show where plaque is building up.

These foods are soaked in fat or oil. Even if the food itself is good for you, the way it has been cooked ruins its nutritional value and means it is unhealthy.

Obesity

Good friend?

How would you help a friend who was very overweight?

I'd be a good friend and try to be positive about other things.

I would try to get them to see a doctor and get help.

An **obese** person is someone who is very overweight and has a lot of extra body fat. Some people are overweight but not obese. Obese people are at risk of serious health problems. Being extremely overweight is bad for the body and mind. It can make you feel tired and uncomfortable and it can put extra stress on other parts of the body, especially the joints. Obesity in young people can also cause high **blood pressure** and high **cholesterol** levels, liver disease and **diabetes**. In older people it can lead to heart disease, heart failure and bladder problems. All of these problems mean that obesity can shorten your life.

blood pressure   pressure of the blood going around the body; a high blood pressure is dangerous

27th May

I'm feeling so miserable and fed up. I ate a whole cherry pie and three bags of crisps again this evening. I thought it would make me feel better. All the other boys were in the park playing football, but I can't keep up with them and I'm fed up of being goalie all the time. I wish I could play sport like I used to. People have all started calling me names and think I'm a joke. I've never felt this **depressed** before. I just don't know what to do. I'm going to make an appointment with the doctor tomorrow to see if she can help me.

Q&A

Q My grandpa had a **heart attack** last year. What does this mean and how can I help him?

A Heart attacks are caused by many different things. Eating too much fat and not taking enough exercise puts you at higher risk. Why don't you go out for a walk with your grandpa as often as you can? Regular exercise will help him recover.

diabetes   disease where sugar and starch are not absorbed into the body properly

Try not to forget
that big fast-food
companies spend
lots of money on
advertising to
encourage
you to eat
junk food.

▶ Check out
these billboards.
This sort of
media pressure
is no good for
your health!

Fast food

We all enjoy eating fast food. It tastes good, it is
cheap and it is ready in minutes. But fast food
can be bad for us in several ways. It can make us
put on weight and contains very few **vitamins**
and **minerals**. It also contains lots of fat and salt.
Salt increases **blood pressure** which, in turn,
puts extra strain on the heart.

calorie   measures the energy value of food

Some people choose foods that are not good for them because they think it is expensive and time-consuming to buy and cook fresh food. But it is possible to eat delicious and healthy food without spending a lot of time or money. The chart below gives some examples of simple ways to improve your diet.

Deep-fried chicken

This plate of chicken and chips looks tasty. But a lot of fat and salt have been used to fry the food.

Choice one

- Chips are cheap, easy and quick to buy and eat.
- Cakes are so delicious after a meal.
- Fizzy drinks are sweet and fun.

Choice two

- Jacket potatoes are not cooked in fat and can cook in the oven while you get on with other things.
- Fruit gives you loads of vitamins and minerals and is thirst-quenching too.
- Water has no **calories**, no sugar, is good for your body and is really refreshing.

Chicken and chips:
Fat   22 grams
Salt 1250 milligrams

Comfort eating and drinking

Michelle was worried about her eating habits. She decided to write a diary to try and work out why she **binges**.

Sometimes I eat if I'm bored and on my own, even when I'm not hungry.

I sat and ate a whole bar of chocolate this evening, just because I was bored. I can't believe it. I was going to go for a swim, but I couldn't be bothered and now I feel sick and fat. This is the second time I have binged this week. Why do I do it? I don't understand. I wasn't even hungry. Next time I feel like stuffing my face with bad food I must make myself go out and keep busy, or at least eat something that's healthy. Then I won't be tempted to eat rubbish.

I don't notice how much I eat. I think it's when I am depressed or lonely. It seems to pass the time.

When I'm upset, stressed out or bored I tend to eat. Because I eat so much I feel bad and eat even more to make myself feel better. It doesn't work though. Sometimes I feel like I've eaten so much that I might as well keep on eating. It's a vicious circle.

addiction   difficult to live without

Alcohol

Some people think that drinking alcohol makes them feel better when they are bored or miserable. But alcohol can make you feel more **depressed** and it is very **addictive**. It also contains a lot of **calories** which will make you put on weight.

▼ Think of something you can do to distract you from bingeing – try going for a walk or swim, or eating some fruit.

Bored?

When you are bored or fed up...

Phone a friend for a chat.

Go for a walk, a swim or a bike ride.

Go shopping with a friend.

Try to resist the biscuit tin.

binge   eating or drinking a lot in one go

There are more obese people in the world than ever before because of all the junk food we eat and all the sitting down we do.

Get active

When Jerome was 15 his doctor told him that his heart was under a lot of pressure because he was **obese**. He weighed 20 kilograms more than he should have done. This put stress on all his **organs** and it stopped him from doing simple things like running up the stairs. Jerome was also very unhappy. 'I was so fed up with myself. People were constantly calling me names because I was fat.' His doctor suggested some exercises, which included walking to school. When he took the bus, Jerome got off one stop early and walked the rest of the way. He started to take the stairs and not the lift or escalator.

Jerome could not believe the difference a bit of regular exercise made. He started cycling at the weekends and now he often goes swimming. His doctor is very impressed, she says, 'Jerome has worked really hard to make a difference and he can see the results. He is so much happier and certainly a lot healthier than when I first met him. He has proved that the combination of a **balanced diet** and regular exercise is the best way to get healthy.'

◀ If you are not used to doing a lot of exercise, try easing yourself into it with regular brisk walks or short bicycle rides.

Q I am overweight and I hate it. I have tried really hard to eat fewer sweets and chips, but I haven't lost much weight. Any ideas?

A It is great that you are eating a healthier diet. Now what you need to do is get some exercise. How about swimming, walking, cycling or playing a sport like tennis with your friends?

Dieting

People diet for different reasons. Some people diet because they want to be in top condition to play sport. Others diet because they think it will make them look good and feel better about themselves. Sometimes people go on a **crash diet** to lose weight quickly for a party or holiday. This is not good for you because you lose weight too quickly. As soon as you stop the diet you put weight straight back on, and sometimes even more.

▼ People come in all shapes and sizes – this is a good thing!

❛You should only be dieting if you are overweight. You can find out if you are a healthy weight by going to see your doctor. We talk to teenagers all the time about things that are on their mind. ❜

crash diet   eating as little as possible in order to lose weight in a short space of time

Lots of changes happen to your body as you grow older and this can make you feel very **self-conscious**. Between the ages of nine and sixteen, most teenage girls experience body changes. Their hips broaden and their breasts develop. Sometimes it is hard to see your body as it actually is, and you wish you looked like someone else. Models in magazines look very thin, but normal healthy people are not like this. Everyone has a different body shape. It is much better to be happy at a healthy weight than to be too thin and unhealthy.

I feel so fat and ugly, I don't like any of my clothes anymore. I feel like I'm never going to get a boyfriend. I'm going to go on a diet tomorrow.

If I was skinnier I'd be happier – I haven't got a boyfriend because I'm fat.

Don't be so stupid. You're not fat at all and you're really pretty. Just stop being so **obsessed** with how you look. I bet the boys will start liking you then – you're really good fun when you're not worrying about your weight.

self-conscious   concerned about how you look

The only way to lose weight successfully is by losing weight slowly, eating sensibly and exercising regularly.

▶ ▶ ▶ ▶ ▶ ▶ ▶ ▶

Go to pages 52 to 53 to find organizations that can give you lots of healthy eating tips.

Dream diets?

There always seems to be a new diet that promises to make all your dreams come true. Most of them do your body no good at all. Sometimes people lose weight for the first week or so, but after that it is not a successful or healthy way to maintain a good weight.

One more spoonful of this soup and I'll be ill!

The no carbohydrates diet

Dear diary – 19 June
I think that this is the diet for me. All I have to do is cut out all **carbohydrates** and fruit and eat loads of cream and meat.

Two weeks later...
Last week I noticed that I was losing weight – hurray! But I've stopped losing weight now and I'm really sick of fatty foods. This diet is disgusting and it makes my breath smell. I'm giving it up.

The spinach soup diet

Great – I've got a new diet to try out. This time I'm sure it'll work. I can eat as much spinach soup as I want, so it must be healthy. I should lose 4.5 kilograms in the first week.

Two weeks later...
I'm always going to be fat – I just felt starving and bored on the spinach soup diet. I lost a bit of weight, but put it straight back on again. Why can't I find something that will keep the weight off forever?

Ex-dieter
Crash diets are no good for long-term weight loss. Listen to this ex-dieter's opinion:

I've followed so many stupid diets over the years and they've never really worked. Most of them made me feel ill because I had to eat such silly things. I've realized that being healthy is much more important.

Recipe

Why not try this healthy fruit cocktail?

1 ripe mango
12 grapes
10 strawberries
1 large banana
juice of a lemon

1. Chop up the fruit into bite-size pieces.
2. Place them in one large bowl, or small bowls for your friends.
3. Squeeze lemon juice over the fruit.
4. Serve with yogurt, if you like.
5. Eat your juicy fruit cocktail and enjoy.

Help!

Dear Prya,
I'm going to a party in two weeks time. My favourite dress is too tight for me now, and I want to fit into it. I've heard there is a quick-fix diet called 'the peanut butter sandwich diet'. Do you think this will work? I really need to lose the weight quickly. All my friends will be at this party and I want to look good. Most of all though, the boy I fancy from school will be there, and I want to ask him out.
Please help me.
Karen

Dear Karen,
Everyone feels **self-conscious** at your age and wants to look good. But I'm afraid these 'dream' diets don't work. They might make you lose weight quickly, but it never lasts. You end up putting more weight on in the end. I would suggest that for the two weeks leading up to the party you try to eat less fat and sugar, lots of fruit and vegetables and exercise about three times a week. In the long term, remember that you need a healthy balance of all food groups.
Prya

Sporty

This sportsman eats healthily to give him energy for his sprinting.

I don't really need to worry about what I eat because I do so much exercise and burn off lots of **calories**. I do eat healthily though, and follow the rules of the food pyramid. I make sure I eat lots of fruit and vegetables, and **carbohydrates**.

A balanced life

To have a happy and healthy life, you need a good mix of healthy food, lots of exercise and good times with your family and friends. At your healthiest weight, you should feel and look good, have lots of energy and enjoy life. The only way to do this is to use common sense and think sensibly about your health. Remember that everyone is different and you should not compare yourself to others. Check out the points opposite. They will help you achieve the right balance.

Keep it simple

To stay at my healthiest weight, I have to eat sensibly and remember to exercise as well.

People who diet have got it all wrong. Why don't they just eat good food, not snack too much and do plenty of exercise?

▶ Exercise about three times a week and try to eat five portions of fruit and vegetables every day.

Eat **carbohydrates** to give you energy.

Eat at least five portions of fresh fruit and vegetables every day.

Protein from meat, fish and dairy products helps you to grow and gives you strength.

Try not to have too many sugary sweets, cakes or drinks, or too many fatty foods.

Exercise about three times a week.

Find an exercise or sport that is fun and that you can do with friends.

Fit exercise into your day so you have the time and energy to do it regularly.

Heart and soul

Recipe for a healthy, happy day.
All you need is:

- great food (a healthy diet)
- a fun sport to do with your mates – how about skateboarding?
- time out to relax and have a laugh
- enough energy so that you can do it all again tomorrow!

Eating disorders

Out of control

Some teenagers find it difficult to come to terms with their body changes during **puberty**. You can feel that you have no control over the way you look.

It is very important to eat a healthy diet and to exercise during puberty. Your body needs help to become strong and healthy.

Some teenagers find it hard to control their eating. People who eat far too much suffer from a **compulsive** eating disorder. Some people make themselves sick after eating. This is called bulimia. People who are not eating enough may be suffering from anorexia. These eating disorders are caused by lots of different things and can affect both girls and boys. Most sufferers feel out of control and might have problems at home or school. People with eating disorders are often very **depressed**. Whatever the reason, these problems are serious and if you or your friend are suffering, you need to get help – quickly.

laxatives   substance that loosens the waste in your bowels and makes you go to the toilet

People often think that those suffering from eating disorders are **obsessed** with the way they look, and sometimes they are. But often the problem is much more serious than this.

> **Anorexia:** sufferers starve themselves and become obsessed with eating only very small amounts of food. People with anorexia look in the mirror and see a fat person, even though they are usually very thin.

> **Bulimia:** people with bulimia eat large amounts of food – this is called **bingeing**. Then they **vomit** and use **laxatives** to lose weight. It is often hard to notice people who have bulimia because their weight is usually average or above average.

> **Compulsive overeating:** an **addiction** to food. Sufferers often feel lonely and may eat food to make themselves feel better.

TRUE OR FALSE?

'Eating disorders just go away by themselves.'

FALSE

People with eating disorders are ill and need a lot of help to make them better. They should start by talking to a doctor who will support them and probably suggest that they see a trained **counsellor**.

Need help?

If you or a friend have any problems with eating, or feel very fed up with life, you should seek help now. Try:

- contacting an organization (see pages 52 to 53)

- talking to your parents or other people in your family

- having a chat with one of your teachers

- seeing a doctor.

Anorexia

Tom was twelve years old when he became really aware of his body and the way he wanted it to look. Lots of things were changing in his life. He was going through **puberty** and his parents had just split up. He had moved away from his friends and he felt very lonely. He wanted to feel in control of one part of his life, so he started dieting to control his weight. He skipped meals and hid food so he did not have to eat it. As the weight dropped off, he felt more confident about himself, even though he was always tired.

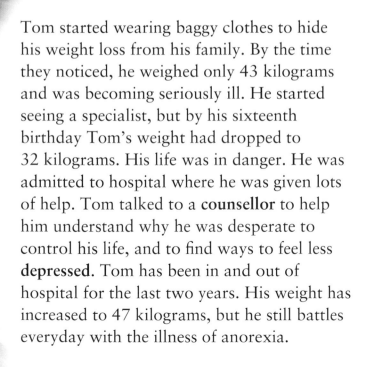

▶ Worried about an eating disorder? Tell someone, talk about it and share your problem.

Tom started wearing baggy clothes to hide his weight loss from his family. By the time they noticed, he weighed only 43 kilograms and was becoming seriously ill. He started seeing a specialist, but by his sixteenth birthday Tom's weight had dropped to 32 kilograms. His life was in danger. He was admitted to hospital where he was given lots of help. Tom talked to a **counsellor** to help him understand why he was desperate to control his life, and to find ways to feel less **depressed**. Tom has been in and out of hospital for the last two years. His weight has increased to 47 kilograms, but he still battles everyday with the illness of anorexia.

Be aware

These could be signs of an eating problem:

- trying to skip meals

- feeling guilty about eating a biscuit

- feeling uncomfortable eating with your family

- thinking your body is disgusting.

Bulimia

Dear Diary

I had a big **binge** today. I've eaten five bags of crisps, a big bar of chocolate, a bag of peanuts, three doughnuts, a plate of chips, as well as my breakfast, lunch and dinner. I feel disgusting again and I made myself sick three times. My stomach is hurting and I've got a horrible taste in my mouth. I can't concentrate at school because I spend all my time planning what I can eat. I don't know why I do it. I read about something called bulimia in a magazine. I think that is what I might have. Maybe I should try to talk to Mum about it.

Spying game

My friend used to eat loads and loads but never put on weight. I noticed that she always went to the toilet straight after eating, and one day I followed her and heard her being sick. In the end she went to the doctor and now she doesn't do it anymore. I'm glad I made her see the doctor and tackle the problem.

decay rot

I used to have bulimia. I would eat and eat and then make myself sick, sometimes five times a day. It was horrible. It took me a while to get better, but my family, friends and doctor all helped me. My doctor warned me that I could damage my stomach and kidneys and may even suffer from heart problems. He also said that the acid in the **vomit** would cause my teeth to **decay**. I'm so much better now. I eat three meals a day, with only a few snacks in between and I exercise twice a week. Anyone who is suffering should speak to their doctor. I did, and it made all the difference.

Sound familiar?

Does anyone you know:

- Go to the bathroom straight after eating?

- Eat huge amounts of food, but not put on weight?

- Think about food all the time?

- Make themselves sick or use **laxatives**?

If so, they might have an eating disorder and need to see a doctor.

Special diets

Many people have special diets, sometimes by choice and sometimes to help them live with certain conditions.

Diabetes

Group talk

I hated being diabetic to begin with. Then I realized that loads of people suffer from it and I joined a 'diabetes friends' group. The group helps me to think about what I can do to control my blood sugar levels and makes me feel normal. You can get special foods for diabetics these days.

I knew I was ill, but I thought it was just **puberty**. I felt tired all the time, but the real giveaway was that I was so thirsty and couldn't stop going to the toilet. When my doctor told me I had **diabetes**, I was so shocked. I didn't really know anything about it. He explained that when we eat, our bodies take the sugar from the food into our bloodstream. This blood sugar is then taken to our cells by something called **insulin** so that our bodies can use the energy. When someone has diabetes, their body cannot make insulin, or cannot use it properly.

insulin   substance made in the body that controls the levels of sugar in the blood

Because I cannot control my blood sugar level, I have to make sure I check it at least four times a day. I have to prick my finger and check the blood on a monitor. I inject myself with insulin to balance it out. Sometimes I feel dizzy or faint, and I can't eat sweets and chocolate like my friends. I was really angry at first and sometimes pretended that I didn't have diabetes. I just wanted to be normal like everyone else. My mum was always checking up on me and that drove me mad, even though I knew she was just worried about me.

▼ This girl is using a **novopen** to inject insulin.

'You can catch diabetes from someone.'

FALSE

Doctors do not fully understand how someone develops diabetes, but diabetics often have the condition in their family. Blood tests are often used to test for diabetes.

novopen pen-like tool that measures out exactly the right amount of insulin

Attack

What should I do if someone I know has an attack because of a food allergy?

• Call the emergency services immediately.

• Explain what you think has set off the reaction.

The right treatment can then be given and the effects of the reaction minimized.

Food allergies

Some people's bodies think that certain foods are trying to attack them. Their **immune system** sends out signals to fight these foods.

The signals make the body release chemicals such as **histamine**. This can cause all sorts of reactions, including; rashes, itchy skin and even breathing difficulties. More serious reactions to foods are called **anaphylactic** food allergies. These reactions can make a person go into shock and lose **consciousness**. People who suffer from this often carry medication with them to take in an emergency.

▼ People can be **allergic** to foods such as eggs, nuts, milk, wheat and shellfish.

anaemia   lack of iron in the body
anaphylactic   life-threatening allergic reaction

Coeliacs disease

To... | Greg
Cc... |
Subject: | Coeliacs

Dear Greg,
My mum has just been diagnosed as having Coeliacs disease. Can you please tell me more about it?
Alan

To... | Alan
Cc... |
Subject: | Coeliacs

Dear Alan,
Your mum is suffering from a life-long condition that makes her body react badly to **gluten**. When someone has Coeliacs disease, gluten damages the lining of their small **intestine** and it can be difficult for them to absorb enough **nutrients**. Gluten is found in cereals and grains, and foods such as bread and pastry. People with Coeliacs disease often have **anaemia**, painful stomach aches and diarrhoea. The only way to treat this is by eating a gluten-free diet. Luckily there are lots of foods that you can now buy that have been made without gluten.

Q&A

Q What is the difference between a food allergy and a **food intolerance**?

A A food intolerance means that the body does not like the food, but the immune system does not send out signals to fight it. People with a food intolerance can usually eat a little of the food they are intolerant to without reacting.

▶ If you eat too much of a food you are intolerant to, you may get stomach cramps.

---

gluten substance present in grains such as wheat
immune system part of your body that fights illness and disease

43

Vegetarianism

Veggie or
vegan?

What is the
difference between
a vegetarian and
a vegan?

Dear health page,
I want to become a **vegetarian** because I think
it's horrible to kill animals for food. My dad is
worried that I won't get enough protein and
iron if I stop eating meat and fish. How can I
convince him this won't happen?
Ben

Dear Ben,
Lots of people are vegetarian and live very healthy
lives. However, you do need to make sure you get
all your **nutrients**. *You can get protein in your diet*
by eating lots of beans, nuts and **pulses**, *like lentils.*
You can find iron in fresh green leafy vegetables.
It's also a good idea to talk to your doctor, who can
give you more advice.

A vegetarian does
not eat meat or
fish, but eats dairy
products such as
milk and cheese.
A vegan does not
eat meat, fish, eggs
or dairy products
and has to get
protein from beans,
nuts and pulses.

vegan   someone who chooses not to eat meat, fish,
eggs or any dairy products

Religious diets

Some people do not eat certain foods because of their religious beliefs.

Jewish people follow these rules for eating:
- they only eat kosher food – food that has been prepared in a special way
- they only eat animals with split hooves that chew grass, so no pork
- they never have milk and meat together
- they only eat fish that have scales and fins, so no shellfish
- they do not eat birds of prey.

Muslims only eat meat and animal fat that is halal. This means that it has been killed in a certain way. They cannot eat pork, sausages or eel and they should not drink any alcohol.

Many Hindus are vegetarian, so they do not eat any meat or fish at all.

Enjoy being different

Some of my friends are Jewish and they eat different food to me. At first I thought it was strange, but now I'm used to it.

Some people are really rude about the food I eat, because I'm Hindu and don't eat meat. It makes me really cross.

I think we should all respect other people's religious beliefs. Being different makes the world more interesting.

◀ Hindus believe that the cow is a holy animal and will not eat any product from it, like beef.

Diet and lifestyle

'Cereal bars are really good for you, they do not have any sugar or fat in them.'

FALSE

Cereal bars contain a lot of hidden sugar. You should always check the labels on your food.

Read this A to Z and pick up some useful tips to help you incorporate a good diet and fitness into your daily life.

Active Keeping active and doing exercise will help you keep at a healthy weight.

Balanced diet A diet that has **vitamins** and **minerals**, **carbohydrates**, protein and a little bit of fat will help to keep you in good physical condition.

Caffeine Found in tea, coffee and cola – it is a substance that makes you feel full of energy for a short time. Try not to drink too much of it.

Dancing A great way to exercise – get all your friends together and boogie on down!

Energy foods Pasta, bread and potatoes all contain carbohydrates that give you slow-releasing energy.

Food labels Look out for labels on all food packaging. They will tell you what the food contains and how much fat it has.

Green vegetables These contain a lot of vitamins and minerals – eat lots of them.

additives   added to food to preserve, flavour or colour it

Hygiene   Keeping clean will help to stop you getting germs. It is also important to keep kitchen surfaces clean when you are preparing and cooking food.

Illness   People become ill when they do not eat a **balanced diet**. It is good to eat lots of vitamin C when you have a cold.

Junk food   Tasty and easy, but full of fat and unnatural **additives**. You should try not to eat too much junk food.

Kiwi fruit   A great source of vitamin C.

Low fat foods   Some foods say that they are low fat, but you need to be careful and look at the label to find out how much fat the food actually contains.

Minerals   Natural substances found in foods such as milk, cheese, fish and leafy vegetables. Calcium is a mineral, which helps to keep your bones healthy.

80% FAT FREE

▲ Be careful when you see this on food packaging.

How healthy?
Even if something is 80 per cent fat free, it still contains 20 per cent fat – and that is a lot! Foods that contain 10 per cent fat or less are usually fairly healthy.

A to Z continued...

Nuts   An excellent source of protein that make a quick and easy snack.

Organs   Your heart, lungs, stomach and brain are all **organs** that make your body work. You can keep them healthy by eating a **balanced diet** and exercising.

Preparing food   The way you cook and prepare food is often the difference between it being good for you or not. Grill or bake foods rather than frying them. This way you use less fat.

Quick snacks   Healthy quick snacks include; a raw carrot, a handful of raisins, any fruit, pitta bread and low fat cream cheese or a handful of unsalted peanuts.

Roughage   Roughage is found in foods that have not been processed, such as wholemeal bread, wholemeal rice, fruit and vegetables. They help your **digestion** and make you go to the toilet regularly.

Salmonella   **Food poisoning** caused by eating raw chicken or eggs that can make you feel very ill. Make sure you keep your cooking area clean and cook your food properly.

Out and about

When I'm busy, I don't have time to make myself healthy food.

I make sure I've got healthy snacks in my bag, so that I'm not tempted to buy crisps and sweets.

When we go out for a pizza, I always have one with vegetables on - it's much healthier.

food poisoning   illness caused by germs in food

Takeaway These meals are often cooked in fat and contain lots of salt and sugar. Try to make time to prepare your own food so that you know what is in it.

Use-by date Labels on food tell you the date the food should be eaten by. When the food is out-of-date it should be thrown away.

Vegetarians People who do not eat meat and get their protein from eggs, cheese, beans, nuts and **soya**.

Water The healthiest drink you can have – full of goodness and nice and cheap. Drink at least five glasses a day.

E**X**ercise Try to do this three times a week. What exercise do you do?

Yo-yo dieting This is when people constantly stop and start diets. It is not a good way to approach long-term weight loss.

Zzzzzzzz Your body does most of its growing when you are asleep. You also need to sleep in order to learn and be alert in the daytime. Because your mind is so active, it is only fair that you give it a chance to rest.

Doctor
I always tell my athletes that there are three things to remember:

- eat a balanced diet

- get lots of exercise

- have plenty of rest and sleep.

◄ ◄ ◄ ◄ ◄
Go to pages 8 and 9 to find out more about a balanced diet.

soya bean you can cook and eat, or crush to make oil

I used to go on those silly diets, but I'd always put the weight back on. I feel much better now that I eat a variety of foods and do exercise too.

Look after yourself

What you eat is really important if you want to grow into a fit and healthy adult. In your teens your body is continually changing. Sometimes you will feel very aware of how you look and how you are different from other people. This is normal – try not to let it worry you too much.

It's really important to have a balanced diet - those crash diets just don't work.

Stupid diets and **crash diets** only work in the short term. They can seriously damage your body and your growth. Look at page 52 for details of books and websites that give lots of ideas for healthy eating.

I love junk food, but I know that it contains loads of fat – eating ice cream is such a treat.

Fruit is a really good snack and it's fast food too.

Chips

'I love chips, but I only have them once a week. I make sure I eat loads of vegetables too.'

Find out more

Organizations

Children with diabetes
A special website for young people with diabetes, where they can share stories and make friends.
childrenwithdiabetes.com

Lifebytes
A fun and informative website that gives young people information to help them make their own choices about their life.
lifebytes.gov.uk

Nutrition Australia
A great all-round reference website.
nutritionaustralia.org

Nutrition UK
Interesting overview of a variety of health issues, including a 'diet through life' section.
nutrition.org.uk

Books

Body Needs: Carbohydrates, Jillian Powell (Heinemann Library, 2003)

Body Needs: Vitamins and minerals, Jillian Powell (Heinemann Library, 2003)

Need to Know: Eating disorders, Caroline Warbrick (Heinemann Library, 2002)

World Wide Web

If you want to find out more about **diet**, you can search the Internet using keywords like these:
- 'balanced diet'
- food + intolerance
- vegetarian
- saturated + fat

You can also find your own keywords by using headings or words from this book. Use the search tips opposite to help you find the most useful websites.

Search tips

There are billions of pages on the Internet so it can be difficult to find exactly what you are looking for. For example, if you just type in 'diet' on a search engine like Google, you will get a list of more than 17 million web pages. These search skills will help you find useful websites more quickly:

- Know exactly what you want to find out about first
- Use simple keywords instead of whole sentences
- Use two to six keywords in a search, putting the most important words first
- Be precise – only use names of people, places or things
- If you want to find words that go together, put quote marks around them, for example 'balanced diet' or 'food intolerance'
- Use the advanced section of your search engine.

Where to search

Search engine

A search engine looks through the web and lists the sites that match the words in the search box. They can give thousands of links, but the best matches are at the top of the list, on the first page. Try searching with **www.bbc.co.uk/search**

Search directory

A search directory is like a library of websites. You can search by keyword or subject and browse through the different sites like you would look through books on a library shelf. A good example is **www.yahooligans.com**

Glossary

addiction cannot live without

additives added to food to preserve, flavour or colour it

allergic have a strong reaction against something

anaemia lack of iron in the body

anaphylactic life-threatening allergic reaction

balanced diet eating a good range and mixture of foods from all the different food groups

binge eating or drinking a lot in one go

blood pressure pressure of the blood going around the body; a high blood pressure is dangerous

calorie measures the energy value of food

carbohydrates foods such as bread, potatoes, rice and cereals that provide the body with a source of energy

cholesterol fatty substance made by the body that can block the arteries to and from the heart, causing heart disease

compulsive when you regularly make yourself do something; you are often not aware you are doing it

consciousness being awake and aware of your surroundings

counsellor someone who will listen to you if you need to talk and offer you practical advice

crash diet eating as little as possible in order to lose weight in a short space of time

decay rot

depressed unhappy and gloomy

diabetes disease where sugar and starch are not absorbed into the body properly

digest to break food down in the stomach, so that it can be absorbed into the blood

floss soft thread used to clean between the teeth

food intolerance when the body reacts badly to a certain type of food

food poisoning illness caused by germs in food

gluten substance present in grains such as wheat

heart attack sudden failure of the heart

histamine chemical released into the body to fight things in the bloodstream

immune system part of your body that fights illness and disease

insulin substance made in the body that controls the levels of sugar in the blood

intestine long tube that carries food from your stomach to your anus

laxatives substance that loosens the waste in your bowels and makes you go to the toilet

minerals simple substances found naturally in the Earth – they can help build your body and keep it healthy

monounsaturated fat fat that the body needs

novopen pen-like tool that measures out exactly the right amount of insulin

nutrients parts of food which the body needs for energy or to build new cells

obese very overweight

obsessed when you cannot stop thinking about something

organs internal parts of your body that are essential for you to stay alive, such as heart, lungs and kidneys

plaque coating that builds up on teeth when bacteria has not been cleaned off properly

polyunsaturated fat fat found in vegetable oils that the body needs

puberty changes that happen to young people as they grow into adults

pulses seeds of plants such as peas, beans and lentils, which are eaten as food

saturated fat animal fats that are used to make cakes, biscuits and other sweet products – they are not good for you

self-conscious concerned about how you look

soya bean you can cook and eat or crush to make oil

supplements tablets or drinks taken to enhance certain parts of your diet

vegan someone who chooses not to eat meat, fish, eggs or any dairy products

vegetarian someone who chooses not to eat fish or meat

vitamins chemicals that the body needs to stay healthy

vomit to be sick

Index

Titles in the *Teen Issues* series include:

Hardback   1 844 43142 8

Hardback   1 844 43146 0

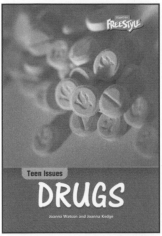

Hardback   1 844 43144 4

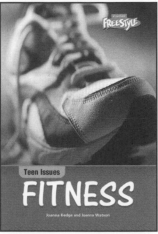

Hardback   1 844 43145 2

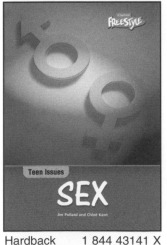

Hardback   1 844 43141 X

Hardback   1 844 43143 6

Find out about the other titles in this series on our website www.raintreepublishers.co.uk